Offerings of Desire

POEMS

KELLY NORMAN ELLIS

Detroit, Michigan

Offerings of Desire

Willow Books
www.WillowLit.com
Willow Books, a Division of Aquarius Press
PO Box 23096
Detroit, MI 48223
www.aquariuspressbookseller.net

Randall Horton, Editor
Cover design by Aquarius Press
Cover art by Krista Franklin

ISBN 978-0-9852877-1-9

Library of Congress Control Number: 2012933059

Printed in the United States of America

I come like a woman
who I am
spreading out through nights
laughter and promise
and dark heat
warming whatever I touch
that is living
consuming
only what is already dead.

~Audre Lorde

Acknowledgments

I bow deeply and humbly to the members of my word/artist family: Dr. Randall Horton and Heather Buchanan; The Affrilachian Poets; The Conjure Women (Parneshia Jones and Ellen Hagan); The Daughters/Sistas (Iman Byfield, Amaris Howard, Adena Washington, Keli Stewart and April Gibson); Cave Canem and their lovely home for Black poetry; artist/conjureman Stephen Flemster and finally the magic ju-ju seer and afro punk Krista Franklin.

To Kevin and Naomi Baskins; the Mobley family of North Carolina; my Slaughter, Ellis and Norman people; my sister Crystal Ellis; the men children (Ellis and Everett Walker); and always, Mama (Cheryl Slaughter Ellis): you are my house, my church of family. Palms together and head bowed, I thank you.

The following poems have appeared in the following journals and anthologies:

Crab Orchard Review: "Affrilachian"

44 on 44: Forty-Four African American Writers on the Election of Barak Obama: "Crossing Over: Invocation for the New Flag"

Reverie: "Ode to Harold's Chicken" and "The Sow"

Rumpus: "Superhero"

Sou'wester: "Shango on the One"

Torch: Poetry, Prose and Short Stories by African American Women: "New Orleans Chant" and "Pontchartrain"

The Ringing Ear: Black Poets Lean South: "Dirty Rice"

Contents

Altars

Superhero	9
Affrilachian	11
Afro	13
Chores	14
Nocturne One	16
Leather Jacket	17
The Sow	19
Phrenology	21
Earth	22
Crossing Over	23
Bill Withers	25
Flag	26
Blue Light Alchemy	28

Second Line

New Orleans Chant	31
Omen	33
Pontchartrain	34
Shango on the One	38
Turning the Body Loose	40
Offerings of Desire	42
Dirty Rice	43
Nocturne Two	44

A House is a Church

Coupled	47
A House is a Church	48
Return Policy	50
What Saves Us	52
Where the Day Leads	53
Ode to Harold's Chicken	54

Her Blue Kitchen   56
Everyone Inside Me is a Bird   58
The Epistles   59
Bodies   62
Linea Nigra   64
Amnesty   65
Naomi Listens to Nina Sing   66
Naomi Listens to Tammi and Marvin   67
Chain Stitch   68
Bread   71
Someplace   72
About the Poet   74

Altars

Superhero
(for Tricia and Bianca)

Lasyrenn's hair
like a rope,
my locks are the new golden lasso.
i am Oya rocking hurricanes.
i am the protector of your dead.
my mother is Marie Laveau
my daddy Stagolee
i am the earth shaker
protector of women
do u know me?
I'm your mother.
say my name
virago
bitch
shrew.
i am the squatting
goddess
Supergirl
not a white chick in tights but
the real one-breasted amazon
riding a black unicorn.
protector of all the scribbling women
in attics
the one who comes when you call
me.
like Eartha's Catwoman
flirt, tease, you want me.
I don't have time.
I'm into ruining shit
subverter,
transformer,
liberator of
desire.
defender of drag queens, of the butch and the femme.

i will come when you whisper
in the dark
when you cry
when you scream like your mother did
i will bring you satisfaction
on a platter.
i live in the Chi.
no batmobile
i ride the City of New Orleans
like a bullet between my legs.
i am protector of
cornbread
and 28 days of the moon
of bruised
plum women
the lynched
the raped.
on my cape is a red S
i am the blood
you see when you peel
back skin, the burst of life
in the back of the throat,
the forbidden fruit.
my uncle was Shango
so I am protector
of righteous men.
turn down your volume
listen,
i am protector of black Presidents,
of translucent truth.
steel toe boots, gold tooth
locks hot to the touch
you know me
I am
Sapphire.

Affrilachian

(for the Black Appalachians)

I
is the total black, being spoken
from the earth's inside.
There are many kinds of open
how a diamond comes into a knot of flame
how sound comes into a word, coloured
by who pays what for speaking.
~Audre Lorde

I be a nipple of coal
the savior's blood on dogwood,
the sun bleached blues of cow bones.
I am the hiding places
of slaves and poke sallet.

I praise the sugar tit and the cooling board,
the banjo's black fingers, the winding road
in Bill Wither's voice.
I praise the Ohio's vicious salvation
and *Were you there when they crucified*
our Lord…Were you there?

Praises to Nina and Booker T,
and even Elvis' Cherokee hips.
Praises be to Bessie
and Roberta and
the Lovings' first kiss.

Like the conjure of the blue black granny
or the whereabouts of gypsy graves,
I am sacred.
I am a prayer, a holler, a ginseng root.

I am a secret
like the girl giving birth

in a tobacco field
wet, silent
the lingering sweetness
of Blue Ridge sunrise
surrounding her.

I be that warm
open place
at the root
praise this lovely
black
flame.

Afro

1. nappy funk. head full of kitchen kick back. See Douglass, Frederick
    or Davis, Angela or your daddy back from Vietnam. Also see fist
    pick and wanted poster (Assata) as in *Mama, I'm on the
    Underground Railroad makin' my way to Cuba.*

2. natural. strawberry sheen. aboriginal orb shaped by palm pat
    around its perimeter. worn with hoops on ears, bangles on wrist.
    See Grier, Pam; Dobson, Tamara; Slaughter, Constance (your aunt)
    first black woman graduate of Ole Miss Law School
    as in *A sista with a tapered 'fro don't play.* may also be worn in puffs
    or married to cornrows twa or blowout. See yo mama and everyone
    of your auntees.

3. sly and the family stone, toni morrison, jimi hendrix,
    foxy shebacleopatra jones, elaine brown, the jackson five,
    nikki giovanni, questlove, sweet minnie ripperton, bill cosby
    lucille clifton, the staple singers, john shaft, don cornelius,
    roberta flack, al green, dr. j, baby dread bob marley,
    mary francis berry, wole soyinka, lauren hill, kathleen cleaver,
    bill withers, gwendolyn brooks, shirley chisholm…

4. a root. an arrogant cloud.

Chores

I. The Bathroom

After school, the canister of Comet sat waiting. I would sprinkle the dust
over tub, commode and sink, kicking up green particles like a radioactive cloud.
Round in circles, rubbing away the bathtub ring and the stubble
from my father's beard in the sink. I scrubbed the commode
with a scratchy brush, then flushed the waste of our waste. Turned on
the hot water to scald away the green paste covering white porcelain.
And with the blue bottle of Windex, I buffed away the toothpaste,
shaving cream, dots of Noxzema, from our morning purifications,
then emptied the trash of stained Kleen-x, Q-tips, Kotex.
I was the sweeper of our unclean places.

II. Dishes

Glasses first, forks and knives next, then dishes. By the time the pots
came round, WKXI was blasting Rick James. Mama fussed,
Hurry up, girl. But the request line was on. This is for Stephanie
in Presidential Hills. Got to Be Real. And I am in the Soul Train line,
dish rag in my hand. Washing, drying, putting away. Pouring chicken grease
in the old Crisco can. And then the DJ was spinning
Isaac Hayes...I Stand Accused...the testify line was open...
folks confessing love and sin. Baby I'm sorry...you the only one...
But I was too young for a boyfriend. The dark brown boy in 9th grade
English who I watched in the hall was already driving and never came
to sock hops. He leaned against his locker cocky. His eyes mannish. My want
for him was fuzzy, unsure like the broken suds
from Ivory bubbles brown with dinner's residue. I suddenly remembered
the pot soaking in the sink, got to scrubbing, wounded SOS pad in my hand.

III. Laundry

At sixteen, I loved the quiet of the laundry room. The smell of Tide,
Downy and dryer sheets. Separation of whites and darks.
Jeans and t-shirts. The rest of the apartment complex trusted
the washer and dryer gods and dropped underwear in hot water
with bleach only returning to pour in fabric softener or grab a Coke
from the vending machine. I stayed. A nest of books on the folding table.
Sometimes it was chemistry or geometry, but mostly the comfort
of a library book. I discovered Jane Eyre and Bertha Mason here,
Tar Baby's broken Jadine and Son. Langston Hughes tapped out blues
from washer and dryer here. I remember my parents never came checking
on me those long Sunday hours. Trusting me safe in the spinning of dryers
and the cleansing of books.

Nocturne One

my grandfather listens to country music from a radio above his bed. Hank
Williams' voice all lonesome and curled seeps from speaker. my grandfather
rests in his boxers with closed eyes. Sometimes the windows are open and
curtains swell and bellow with a small pop as they rise then recede. Eyes still
shut he reaches above his head and spins the dial until Fats Domino's voice
creaks through the static. I love my grandfather he is warm and sometimes he
teases and tickles me, sometimes he sings I'm walkin to New Orleanssss.
I listen to crickets or wind or the old oscillating electric fan. mmmmmmmm click
mmmmmmmm click. my grandfather snores inside the opry of night songs.

other rooms have their own night music. the sizzle of hot comb on kitchen eye.
an auntee shakes a pot of popcorn over the stove's blue flame. bursting kernels
between the murmurs of female voices. the opening and closing of the bathroom
door. the gurgle of an empting drain. the flush of commode. womanish laughs.
under the sounds of women, Curtis Mayfield. the running of dishwater. release
of air from a Tab. an auntee pops her knuckles. the steady rock of the washing
machine. cars pass the house with a whoosh of sound, headlights swinging against

the wall. when my grandfather's breath becomes steady, I hear my grandmother's
body bending to pray at the foot of the bed. I love my grandmother. I feel her
hand pressing against the creaking mattress as she lifts herself to rise.

Leather Jacket

I want a leather jacket
make it black like revolution
like Elaine or Kathleen on panther
patrol.

I want a silver scar
rising from
belly to chin
and others slashing the mouths
of my pockets.

I want a pair of gloves to match
tight skin
like new fingers
when I curl them to make a fist.

And I need
an afro
not my faux 'fro ringlets
new millennium style
but my mother's 'fro.
Elegant wild
tapered in back
lined up
shit kicker
on a WANTED
poster
'fro.

I will wear my jacket, my gloves, my afro
to grocery stores
and my daughter's school.
A little bit of fear rising
from the butcher
when I buy the pot roast

or my daughter's teacher
on report card day.

I may be a loose cannon
a little bit crazy
violent
unpredictable.
How would they know?

The Sow

When I was ten
I watched my grandfather
and the men who worked for him
silently circling the body of a sow.
She hung from a hook hoisted
to a tree near the barn.
I remember my grandfather's
back to me and when he turned
there was a piglet floating
in his hand. My grandfather
held the sack of fetus like
a weight. I stared at the sow's
exposed insides revealing
more of her dead children.

In memory, my grandfather's face
is still mystery to me. He and his
men all head bowed as if waiting
for God's rebuke. One man twisted
his stained cap in his hand.
I wonder if my grandfather
mourned the mother?
Her family's death by his
design.

Poor critter,
dying for her salty skin
and innards.
I think of her today
as the news tells of pandemic
named in her honor.
Now, we say she floats
in our lungs
sickening the world.
Oh my sister, it is not you,

but our own
fearsome,
murderous,
love.

Phrenology
(for Crystal)

Her eye catches the way
threads of hair bend and hold

light in a wave. She has always
known where root will send curl

how to listen for music in
the tight compression of braids.

Baby hair is best whispered down
with a toothbrush, and she dreams

of honey hovering your head
like some women foretell futures.

 Ah, and it all comes
so easy how she touches

the frayed ends of ends.
A phrenologist's hands

feeling the beauty
hidden and rising

from our skins.

Earth

Because your grandparents
are earth now, you remember
you and your grandmother quiet together.
you don't remember how old
you are in the backyard
when she shows you the blackberries growing
along the road. you can't recall her words
but you can feel
her guiding your hand between the briars
and the dirt
and somewhere   you know love
is made of growing places
when you and your
aunt walk between rows of greens. you are very small
inside the huge leaves probably collards. you are wearing
a pink dress
and your aunt, you believe it is charlotte, has combed your hair
in two braids.   your grandfather is there.
he takes a picture of you and your aunt   between the rows.
you remember them laughing. you remember she is squatting
close to the ground with you.   there is the smell of earth.   your aunt
says
not to get dirty. says hold the greens in your hand
hold them high for the picture. and then you three walk among
some vines.   and your grandfather loosens the dirt
with one hand unraveling
a clump of peanuts,   hits it against his foot.
your grandfather smells like living things.
like silt.

Crossing Over: Invocation for the New Flag

(November 4, 2008)

This is a new song
for the crossing over.
new anthem,
new banner
to be waved.
here is the new flag embroidered
with Choctaw sassafras root
with Harlem, the Delta, Washington Heights
and every Chinatown everywhere,
the Nigerian girl braiding hair in Chi,
the Eritrean driving a cab in Philly.
this is a flag for the creole of Treme,
the bursting murals of Pilsen
the wings of flying Tuskegee men.
wave this flag like it was never a lie
for those who pray five times a day,
for Bessie Smith's Affrilachian Mountain,
for the American Issei and Nisei,
for Chaney, Goodman and Sherwner,
for Malcolm in his winding sheet
and all the *Native Sons*
Bigger and Medgar and Baldwin and Alexie
for Harvey Milk
and all the ones who can't because
we won't.
for the ones who chanted
Today's a good day to die
for Leonard Peltiter and Wilma Mankiller,
for Robeson and Einstein,
the hustler on the El
and the banger on my corner.
for Ethel Rosenberg in the electric chair.
I am crossing over now
for all Zora's Yoruba Seminole songs,

for Vietnamese shrimpers in Galveston
and Sacagawea and Studs Turkel and
for Denise, Carole, Addie Mae and Cynthia of
Birmingham,
John Reed and Harold Washington,
DuBois and Booker,
Martin, Rosa and Fannie Lou,
for Pete Seeger, Marvin Gaye,
Coltrane, Nina Simone
and all the See Line Women.
this is the crossing over banner
about the Sioux and Chickasaw and Choctaws and
the Hopi and Iroquois and Cherokee,
for all the Hussians and Fatimas,
for Jesus and Esparanza,
for those who sat in
and those who cut down
the lyncher's nooses.
For Matthew Shepard and Ida B.
For Barack and Michelle and Malia and Sasha
opening themselves like soft black wings.
I will fashion a new flag
from the old one folded like a triangle
and buried
in my black grandfather's Mississippi
grave.

Bill Withers

leaves me undone
open
like necking
for the first time
unraveled slow
from an hour
of kissing
he got something
in his voice
like rough wind
like West Virginia
sweat
leaning leaning
against me.

Bill, tell me a story
with your slow threaded
crave
and covet
and that thang
I can't name
but Lord,
I
want.

Flag

(for Sidney Ellis)

Those grammar school mornings
we placed hands over hearts
and recited in small metronomed voices
I pledge allegiance
to the flag
of theUnitedStatesofAmerica.
We chanted
still bruised
from the combing of naps
the rough washing of faces.
The flag
was arrogant,
tense, removed
from our ashy elbows
and knees.
But our forced reverence
was faithful. Every time we heard
the Banner's notes
we stood,
pressed hands to breasts
and mouthed
a song we couldn't sing.

I remember watching
my stepfather at a football game.
Vietnam still in his fists.
He refused to cover his heart.
He leaned into me,
Don't do that unless you mean it,
he said.

I still see him standing
while the marching band crescendoed.
Afro like a sun

the first four buttons of his shirt undone,
blue jean jacket open
black heart exposed.

Blue Light Alchemy

(for Michael Jackson)

a rotation
an orbed
path
inside a circle
inside a
circle
revolutions
into
a groove
worn in the floor
where you
spun
like a
planet
worn
into new element
spun into a black
Saturn
light and gas
into sulfur
blue light
alchemy
a spinning top
of memory
you will
lock and pop
your vinyl self
that sweet tenor
and terror
into the blur
of a black boy's
body.

Second Line

New Orleans Chant

(for Ed Bradley)

you creole
you crazy
carry a razor in your garter
you Shango and blue
you feed women tomatoes
with salt in the dark you Jelly Roll
and Blue Bland you Wynton and Brandford
Papa Ellis too
you like Gumbo for Christmas
grits & oysters for breakfast
chickoree in the coffee
butter on the biscuit
you conked
you waved
you nappy all over
you Yoruba and neckbone
pressed handkerchief in pocket
you wingtipped
you old
you Fats Domino
you a mannish whisper
in married gal's ear
you black as black
you Neville's falsetto
you yellow
you new
you back
you bone
you frazzled tail rooster
you preacher and teacher
you sacred
you dirty profane
you sweet tea in mason glasses
you husband and buttermilk sweet back door man

31

you the moaning in church you the bass at the altar
you latin mass incense Legba riding his horse
you be
Damballah
on the cross

Omen

Blackbirds descended every October
to cover the elm in the side yard.

      We complained
about their stool on our cars. Cursing their stains,
I'd hose down the driveway remembering Hitchcock

and Tippi Hedren's scratched face. Silently the birds
and I watched each other. They were up to no good.

In November, done with their hovering, they moved on.

I am a woman of omens.

      I stay indoors when blood is on the moon, believe
dreams of fish foretell fat babies and the dead talk
      to the living in dreams.

Do blackbirds in trees tell
      of cancer or car wrecks? Of losing
          elders or babies?

You died two Octobers ago, and the birds have refused
to return.

Pontchartrain

(or Okawata to the Choctaw)

I.

Canal to Rampart Street past Church's Chicken
over the Industrial Canal into the Lower Nine
to Holy Cross to St. Barnard's.
This is not the tourist's geography
no Bourbon St. or Rue Royal
no oysters at Antoine's
but empty nail salons and check cashing shops
deserted Chevron's and juke joints named Club Harmann

We are the two headed city
the living covering the dead
the dead hovering the living
always dying
always living
always shit
always jasmine

On the sightseer's map
there are no mildewed American flags
hung in Child Development Centers
for Positive Beginnings,
rancid footballs from the Zulu Krew
only frat boys screaming for naked breasts.

In the Lower Nine, you won't find Jesus,
won't find George W or Nagin,
won't find FEMA,
or Moses,
or Noah,
no Jesus,
but his mother Mary
dots deserted lawns.

She stands
empty palms
up
staring at her sisters across the street.
You won't find Jesus
but you will find a chorus of virgins,
mothers of God.

Hail Mary full of grace
where is your son?
This is the two headed city
the living covering the dead
the dead hover the living
always living
always dying
always jasmine
always shit

II.

Four months before her mouth swallows the city,
I drive across Lake Pontchartrain at 5 am
suspended like a raven in the dark
I leave behind fried pickles in the Irish Channel,
muffalattas and cokes for breakfast, dancing
at Café Negril
and a Spanish balcony on Rampart Street.
It will be good to ride into Pontchartrain's mouth
again. The bridge turns
to Mississippi and I watch the sun
burn away the black morning
New Orleans to my back.

Back in Chicago,
August brings thirsty nights and longing
for Highway 90
for Gulfport, Long Beach, Pass Christian,

Waveland.

August brings Katrina.

Ponchartrain opens herself like a thousand birth waters.
Ponchartrain covers my bridge with her dark slick mouth.

And all my dreams become prayers.

III.

Oshun Yemonja Oya

Reach beyond your many breaths
Beyond ashes and dust
Touch your children
In this sacred place
We will pour honey in your mouths

Oshun Yemonja Oya
Protect the dead and the living
Reveal the pearl beneath the moss
Fill this city with egg and seed
We will pour honey in your mouths.

We are swirling black bodies rising
Land of afterbirth and loas
of clicking tongues
and crescent moonwalk rising

Oya Yemonja Oshun
Three sisters of the storm

Talk to Jesus
Tell him his mothers live here
Tell him his sisters sleep here
between the cities of the dead

and Marginey
between Metarie
and Slidell
between Biloxi
and Waveland

Tell him you are waiting
in the salted
womanwidewaters
of Okwata.

Shango on the One

(for James Brown)

Recognize his foot in patent leather percussion
or in a black man's hip bone
spinning
Call it on the one and watch

as he becomes a helix on ankle bones
for all those black amputations
jubas and cakewalks.

We forgot Shango's name
but not his syncopated thunder
or pulsing slide muscle
or toe grip camel walk.

James,
growl our gods back to us
gutbucket on the one
not the four or the two

Suck it back
heel and toe
bass on the one
not the two or the four

Shango press his foot on your chest
and funk press back.

Wring out them drawers
and fling them
through the pompadour black.

Hammer his name
Shango
on the flame of a night train screaming
in your lungs.

James know Shango live,
on the downbeat
with dice, neckbone, and a slick wave
of grease on his palm.

James,
just bend that mic
back like you kissing
a woman's neck
and let the funk erupt
like it used to do.

Turning the Body Loose

(or a Bop for Oya)

Oya, why won't you leave me be?
I do not care about your bottle tree
of spirits or buzzards with parcels of souls
in their beaks. Girl, go back to your bone yard,
take the pennies from my eyes. I cannot read
the dead.

I went down to St. James Infirmary
see my baby there
stretched out on a long white table
so sweet so cold so fair

Last week, I dreamed of hoot owls and drowning
in muddy water. Last night of red hens crowing
while they crossed dusty roads. Girl, stop sending me
your omens, I cannot read the dead. As a child I played
in cemeteries walking on the graves. Remember, my
offerings of plums to sweeten your twirling tongue? Keep
the dead inside your gates, cause I cannot read the dead.
I cannot read the dead.

Thirteen going to the graveyard
Only twelve coming back
Thirteen going to the graveyard
Lord, only twelve coming back

Oya, don't bring me no more death for a first line dirge.
The moan of *St. James Infirmary* settling in my throat.
I will not read the dead. I won't. I want a second line
parade. *Didn't She Ramble?* from a brass band wind,
spinning umbrella in my hand. Girl, let me turn
the body loose. Let me turn the body loose.

Let her go, let her go let her go wherever she may be,
she will search the whole world over
*But she'll never find another one like me.**

St. James Infirmary Blues

Offerings of Desire

(for Mother Miriam)

The Vodou Spiritual Temple dangles like a kiss
when the bell over the door shivers. The wonderment
of browsing
seducing women from the sidewalk. Voyeurs of the city
browse fake alligator teeth   bottled gris gris.
A woman with altars lives
in this shop of gods on Rampart Street. She knows
the women who will follow
her behind the counter
out the back door
through the courtyard
past the gray cat extending hind leg
to clean her thigh
past a dry fountain
to a room bulging with offering
where the woman with altars enters them
like sweet smoke.

Pregnant mosquitoes bite the women's ankles,
behind their ears.
The altars brim with honey and evaporating perfumes
with mirrors and shells, pennies and cowries
libations of rum and whiskey.
The women's nipples harden.
And they stare
into Oya's mouth
desire in the coil
of their clitorises.

Dirty Rice

With bits of crawfish
the man makes me tremble.
He feeds me the tiny meat.
I taste the salt on his fingers,
and want his cold gin.

At the French Market,
he puts bell peppers to my nose,
presses my finger to eggplant and okra.
Back home he washes two tomatoes in the sink,
sprinkles them with salt and pepper, holds the fruit
to my lips. He says *Bite, Cher.*

On Royal Street, he teaches me to eat
oysters arranged on a plate of crushed ice,
how to spread Tabasco and horseradish on the raw flesh,
and loosen my throat for the slide of muscle,
then chase with the cool yeast of a Jax.

His favorite is the dirty rice
his mama made when he was a boy.
He slices livers and gizzards, drops them in a skillet
of butter and glassy onions. The kitchen table, covered
with shrimp, is a bed of sweet craving.

Nocturne Two (New Orleans Halloween)

(for Dflo)

carnival dream
the four of us masked
on Frenchmen Street
night smells of river
vomit
rum
something fried
in the crush of bodies
and swirl of lights
we all hold hands
snaking through the costumed
street
when our fingers
break
I hold my breath
to my
ribs
ride the pulse of people
against me
the brass band and alcohol
swirling in my head
a drunk man dressed in a kilt with
a dildo reaches for me
you pull me before he can touch
then press your hand to my back
guiding me to the others
I can't see you
this night
but I know
your hand
is there.

A House is a Church

Coupled
(for Susan Harrison)

your father's face lines the white bowl
after you eat grits

your mother's pin curled hair is the moon
the palm of your hand

the egg carton cracked and veined
they raise up from the bulbous places

A House is a Church

a house is a church
on warm days
God enters
in the quiet

and the Jobs and Rachels
living in the walls of your old
house
sway
with begots beholds
and fear nots

a house must be a church
not a trembling place
with wrath
but a home of blood
and worry just the same

mercy is the kitchen
of warm naan
coffee
Sunday stews of lamb and onions
and Sweet Honey in the choir

grace is the porcelain
tub where you lower
for warm baths
a white bar of soap against
your brown stomach
your neck
your legs

and the bed where you rest
under open windows
breeze cooling your body

is the forgiveness of all
is the resurrection

Return Policy

women like us
never give people back

even when you believe
you leave us

there is a bitter
memory or lovely bit

of story
we summon.

we keep the skin
the liver

the spine
never let go

of hair
or foot

or tongue
we never relinquish

our own
kind

you can never return
our lips   eyes

or the cauls we gave
the day you crawled

through   we are
where you are

you do not give
women like us

back.

What Saves Us (after Bruce Weigl)

(For Kevin)

Sometimes it's the messiness.
Fluids and stains of birth
painful and divine.
Other times,
the clean days
of your grandmother hanging
towels on the clothes line. Or
the sparkling surfaces of days,
bedroom windows open,
Stevie singing
*All I do Is Think About
Yooou...*
Sometime it's the dark,
no moonlight, eyes
adjusting to
the gentle surprises of touch
and whisper or
sunlight on April Fridays
when your daughter
masters the art of jump rope,
pink Chuck Taylors
skipping
and then sometimes it is just
the memory of
you
on those Saturday mornings
when we curled for naps
the best of us lying between
our bodies
sleeping.

Where the Day Leads

After she turned her daughter to the morning,
the day led her to rain and books and a sweater.
Her great grandmother's story and a cup of coffee.
And she followed the day like bread crumbs in the forest.
Sleeping and waking, and doing the wash, styling her hair.
Folding the clothes, eating vanilla wafers.

She followed herself in a Lucille Clifton poem
then she wove her way out and turned on the computer,
but decided to clean out her purse instead.
And the day tumbled on.
Small and silent
And the phone never rang so
she played music and tried on old earrings.
She remembered an old Ruth Brown song and played it five times.
Every time it rains I think of you
And the day led her to the memory
of him leaving for work before day. The kiss
and the missing him
even before the door gently shut.

Ode to Harold's Chicken

I realized your divinity
standing in front of the Chicken
Shack, Hyde Park, Chicago.
The woman behind the window
bellowing MayItakeyourorderplease
Saturday night and she has no
patience with the inexperienced.
I hear the orders of the faithful

six wings saltpeppermild
two piece dark saltpepperhot
gizzards saltpepperfried hard
a side of okra
and I choose.

It is the baptising
of chickenwingsfrieswhitebread
with sauce then marriage
of strawberry soda
and freedom burst
of greasy flesh in
my mouth
and I am sanctified.

Holy Harold
Chicken King of the
South Side, patron saint of
fried wings, two pieces,
catfish with hot.

All praises to Saint Harold
cup your hands receive
his holy substance
remembrance
of the deep fried

Saturday night juke,
and Sunday supper,
and
I lick my fingers
with joy.
Oh I am
the devout
sinner and Harold
you make my sin
prayer.

Her Blue Kitchen

(for Agnes Jenkins)

Grandmama's kitchen is the blue note
percussion of pound cake
and pecans
and the pout of my longing
for her bowl and wooden spoon

blues were born on
this red kitchen table
with silver chrome legs
a bowl of eggs
and wax paper circles
She carried
the down beat in her mixing hand
the clicking
of knife on cutting board
pickle and celery
for potato salad
her worry note

tells me what is blue
in syncopations of
the boiling turnip pot
like the train pushing
through yazoo
her work songs
are the cleaning of chitterlings
and the clabber of milk

translates pain
in the grits and gravy deep moan
and the jagged wounds of cracklin' bread
fish grease

the despair of blackberry cobbler
and the seeds in your bad tooth
the black blue of your tongue
your lips.

Everyone Inside Me is a Bird*

While you were still curling
under my heart
keeping yourself secret,

a crow followed me
from the bus stop
to my office one day.

Her beautiful black body
striding behind my heels.
It was late summer,

and I was dizzy with heat,
strings of nausea
unraveling me.

Gypsy bird
cocked her silent head
and mimicked a whisper.

Baby,
Mama is Mississippi raised
by two headed
women and knows

a sign when she sees it.
I knew Sis Crow was telling
of some life crossing,

just didn't know it was yours
beating and fluttering
inside me like wings.

*from "In Celebration of My Uterus" by Anne Sexton

The Epistles

Dear Everett,
You are five and beautiful.
You run fast, spin your
spider man webs. Move
your body like dandelion
spins. You suck your
thumb,
sometimes. You are
all of the time
a strong brave boy.
You are sometimes
naughty. You are
all of the time smart.
You are one of my
favorite things.
The loveliest thing
about you
is the way you love to bake
cakes. White cake with
sprinkles or strawberry
cakes with white icing. Your
great-great grandfather
baked cakes too. He baked
pound cakes that
tasted like almonds or vanilla
and butter. He was
the color of lemons like
you. He would love
the way you bake.
Maybe something inside you
remembers him. Next
time I see you, bake me
a yellow cake. You
can pick the frosting.
Love,
Me

Dear Ellis,
You are beautiful
and five. You like
dinosaurs and computers.
Remember,
when you made me
read the dinosaur book
10 times under the
Christmas tree? How
you taught me to play
Wow Wow Wubbzy? You
are sometimes naughty, but
you are always love. You are strong
and brave and you sing in the shower.
I think
you know magic
things because sometimes,
you tell me secrets without
talking. I like the way
you play with mountains
of bubbles in the tub
and order me to sit
on the floor where warm
water has spilled on the floor.
I don't mind.
You are afraid
of bugs and birds, but not jumping
off your grandmother's bed like
a sky diver. You point your magician's finger
at the globe in the den
and say all the continents
like a song.
You are one of the smartest
people I know. You
are one of my favorite things.

Sometimes when I am sad,
I think of how
you kiss the people you
love and I feel better.
How you press your lips to my
cheeks, your body jumping
up and down like a grasshopper
makes me smile big. Oh,
how your great grandfather would love
that. He loved kissing the people
he loved too. Maybe something
inside you remembers him.
You are a brilliant shiny boy.
Next time I see you, I will
bring you a dinosaur book.
Love,
Me

Bodies

We leave the fancy restaurant downtown
me, my daughter, her father. A birthday celebration
of crab legs, shrimp, hot bread, calamari. A rum and coke for me,
gin and tonic for him, a Shirley temple with lots of cherries for her.
We walk the blocks back to our car and daughter presses her
body close to her father and me. Fear in her hand holding mine,
she sees the body curled between popcorn store and sandwich shop
sleeping over a street grate. The body shifts under a gray tarp. Man
or woman we do not know. And then on State street another body
between the spaces of Macy's sleeping. She shifts into mine, utters a little
groan. She has seen the homeless before. In front of the pizza joint
or the bookstore on 57nd. But it is dark and the bodies are mysteries
without mouths.

II.
The conductor says they must cut off the power to the blue line el.
We exit to an army of police, yellow tape.
The crowd wants to see
the dead
body under the platform. Woman or man
we do not know. They want to witness
the leavings of a life. What will they
find? Eyes?
Toes, dried blood?
A lonely penis?
Breasts?
Maybe a scar without a story.

III'
I have my father's heart which almost exploded
when he was 45. I am 46.
I lay on a table in the room for sonograms
a woman spreads clear
cold jelly over my breast. She rolls her kneading
machine across me. I hear my heart talking.

What she knows is legion.
A murmur at six, the years of bacon grease in Grandmama's
cornbread, how many fried eggs I have eaten. But only she knows
the day she will
decide to quit
her beating. Leaving a
body to its quiet.

Linea Nigra

In my globing belly, you are a continent
shifting your backbone against mine
I am elastic world pulled from
north to south pole
linea nigra stretching
a dark equator parting me
my daughter, you bring
no imaginary line
but you half me
into two hemispheres
body and blood
mother
daughter

Amnesty

I am reading you *The Secret Garden*
under the covers. It is a shivering
April night, and I recall
my old white teacher, Mrs. Greer
who sat before the classroom
and read every day this story.

Some days I felt her turning
away from our small dark faces
ignoring our desires. But in the moment
she sat on her stool, holding the
green book in her hands,
reading of the little girl who brings
a garden to life,
I forgave her like I hope you will
forgive me for all the mother's
turning away I have done.

Now, our faces are under
the down comforter,
me turning the yellowed pages
and your father asleep on the other side.
We are inside the church of each other
and your absolution
saves me again.

Naomi Listens to Nina Sing

This to remind you
of that morning in April when
you were almost nine,
how we rode to the pancake house
before a spring shopping spree.
Do you remember
listening to
Nina sing? How when
we slid into the parking space, you asked
if we could sit and hear the end
of this lady's song
about a bird that had once
been a woman?
you hushed, eyes wandering out
the window when Nina sang with
keys instead of voice.
did you hear water? your great grand
mother's skirt brushing past? my silver
earrings dangling when we hug?
You say, "I want to hear what her piano
is doing."
I said hear baby.
Hear.

Naomi Listens to Tammi and Marvin

(for Kim)

Yesterday, I heard
voices stirring
behind your ten year old
closed door. Clinking bells
and *Listen Babeee*
on this day in June you
are Tammi and Marvin's
love crescendoed in a whirl
of barefooted light,
and you are drunk with tender bass
and Tammi's soprano.
You are feel good
fingersnap.
You are the shivering
tambourine.

Chain Stitch

"Poor people do crochet," sniffed my older sister. "Fine ladies do needlepoint."*
Poor like a scrap quilt, like a country church, like grits and gravy, like wildflowers…

I sit outside the door of my daughter's piano lessons
yarn curled through fingers.
The woman next to me
is my grandmother's same creamy brown,
but she speaks Spanish
to her granddaughter.
One day she brings a bag of yarn
and hooks. Her fingers are faster than mine.
The nuns teach us in Mexico when I am a girl she says.
We speak of shells and picots
of the right kind of yarn
then of how to make hot chocolate properly
all in the language
of loop and chain
a poor woman's tongue

*Poor like neckbones and rice, like food stamps, like government cheese, like clean clothes
on a line, like riding the Greyhound…*

The bus from Lexington to Nashville
stops outside Bowling Green for the black buggy
near the road
a family of red faces waits in the cold
December
the men in black suits
the women white bonnets.
A girl sits in the empty seat beside me
she does not speak, but watches
my hook carry loop through loop
the strands of plain brown hair
peeking through her bonnet.

My hands say, I am a yarn charmer. Her eyes
say *Teach me.*
I raise my hands so she can read,
this old language
After an hour
she falls asleep and
dreams of the stories my hands
tell

*Poor like kitchen beauty shops, like a Simplicity pattern, like Pet Milk in your
coffee, like an unpaid light bill...*

My mother afro wide,
yellow t-shirt
worn jeans
silver bangles bouncing
against her wrist
*Swing the hook back slightly
so that the yarn falls over the hook**
Sometimes her hands are fury
sometimes trance
but later a chain of
color snakes in her lap
*Rotate the hook so the throat faces down
and pull to the right, bringing new yarn
under the old**
Each loop is bill unpaid
another loose thread
my father has left untied.
*Pull a little bit more to the right
and allow the old loop to slip
off the hook**
The red black and green
afghan, the crocheted rounds
inside winter caps,
the scarf for Papa
are the counted stitches
of her worry.

Make the movement a part of your memory*
With each gift, she ties
off her pain
gives it away.

Poor like the blues, like wild turnips, like your grandfather's overalls, like
Vaseline on your knees, poor like a spiritual?

I made this blanket
to keep you warm
all I have is this warm
me
woven into the loops
of this poor yarn
my mother taught me how
to pray this way
mantra of love
through pain
and surrender to
your face when I offer
to you the scraps of me
a poor woman rich
with warm.

*Crocheting in Plain English

Bread

The smell of oranges and cilantro
folds into the grocery bags
and follows me home
from the market where I buy
naan. In my kitchen,
I warm the bread
and spread a thin layer of ghee
on its bubbled skin.
I think of a woman somewhere
who makes her own
bread pressed against an earthen pot.
Is she as fragrant as my hands?

I am the woman who cooks the cornbread
when days are short and dark or biscuits before
the house wakes. My daughter smothers them with
preserves and butter. She eats the warm insides. Her
father is the soft insides of banquettes he uses as extra
fingers to soak up olive oil or the hot lentil soup I make
in winter.

And I think of my mother and grandmother
who taught me to hoard the stale crumbles
of cornbread in the freezer for dressing. Green
onions, bell pepper, eggs, the broth of a hen
and the baking again. I will always love this
more than the turkey. This bread of sage and gravy.
The thankful bread of my mothers.

Bread is the body
we desire
again
memory of eucharist
swallowed sacrifice.

Someplace

(for Amanda Jane Mobley Baskins)

There is a someplace
that reminds you of your first
place
because the people there share
pound cake, peach ice cream,
the promise of memory.
Fish frys in the July backyard
are for new and returned kin
and there is an Aunt Dee
and an Aunt Lily
and an Aunt Bessie
who holds your hand
then whispers *I've known you forever.*
These women are yours
because you remember
auntees and how they love.

Here, uncles smile like sugar,
pat your hand,
want to know about your people.
They are the color of deep open
places.
Here, cousin is a fist of a word
cousin is one who *will fight hurricanes for you,*
cousin is *the one who knows your first names.*

In this someplace, the men quiz
children on who begot them all,
carry in their pockets
prizes for the sacred answers
and drive you to a cemetery like the ones you know
in Mississippi red clay.
And two, more like father and son
than cousins, guide you through the stones

reciting blessed names like prayer.
It is here your daughter and her father
spread his mother's ashes over the ones
who made her.
This moment opens the hundred doors
of your many heart places where family
is the only thing you know.

Now when your daughter's face
changes into a hundred eyes
you will recognize what
is North Carolina carved.
You are grateful this
girl child chose your
body to pass through
sending you here
to this Affrilachian* place.

And you remember
Naomi and Ruth
the old story
you go where she goes
her people
your people.

About the Poet

Kelly Norman Ellis is an associate professor of English and director of the MFA in Creative Writing Program at Chicago State University. She is the author of *Tougaloo Blues* and co-editor of *Spaces Between Us: Poetry, Prose and Art on AIDS/HIV*, both from Third World Press. Her work has appeared in *Crab Orchard Review*, *Sou'Wester*, *PMS (Poem, Memoir, Story)*, *Tidal Basin Review*, *Calyx*, and *The Ringing Ear*. In 2010 *Essence Magazine* voted her one of their forty favorite poets. She is a Cave Canem Poetry Fellow and founding member of the Affrilachian Poets.